DOME.

ST. JOSAPHAT CHURCH
MILWAUKEE WIS.

GNED BY
R & SONS.
& SUPERINTENDENTS

CONSTRUCTED BY
THE J.G.WAGNER COMPANY
MILWAUKEE WIS.

The classic definition of prayer involves the "lifting of the mind and heart to God." Over the millennia of human history we have sought ways and means of entering into the mysterious presence of God. To express the wonder, we have built structures of all sorts to "house the mystery" and articulate the Presence of God dwelling among us. *Ecce! Tabernaculum Dei cum hominibus!* Behold! The dwelling place of God among men! (From the baldachino of the Basilica.)

The heart of the Judeo-Christian notion of Faith reveres that cohabitation of God with us on earth. From the walk in the Garden of Eden, the Ark of the Covenant, and the splendor of Solomon's Temple; to the stable at Bethlehem and the hill of Calvary; to the Major Basilicas of Rome and this Minor Basilica in Milwaukee, humanity celebrates Divine Presence. We do so in art and architecture, stone and steel; in colors of glass and carvings of wood, in silver and gold. The expressions explode with human creative genius striving--crying out--reveling--in efforts to plumb Divine realities.

You are about to enter into a story about such reverence. This book, itself a work of art, tells the history of faith. It reflects the compendium of the impact of that faith on the lives of the faithful and their way of responding to it. The people are God's people, rich in ethnicity and culture, but always God's people. The book is about a living place--an expression of love and devotion that is no less true today than it was 115 years ago when the parish was founded. We are here for a short time; all the while we strive to create a glimpse of our true homeland in Heaven.

Thanks to those who tell the story of the Basilica's faith today and to those whose efforts will continue its reality into tomorrow.

Very Rev. William Patrick Callahan, OFM Conv.,
Rector and Pastor

Introduction

CREDITS

Art Direction, Photography, and Layout
DANIEL BRIELMAIER

Printing Consultant
SCOTT LATUS

Copy
ROBERT FOJUT
JOHN LENCHEK

Managing Editor and Chaplain
REV. MICHAEL J. GLASTETTER, OFM CONV.

Associate Editor
REV. ROBERT JOSEPH SWITANOWSKI, OFM CONV.

Publisher
VERY REV. WILLIAM PATRICK CALLAHAN, OFM CONV.

Additional Photography
BRIAN A. HANSEN
SCOTT LATUS
ERIC OXENDORF
ST. JOSAPHAT BASILICA FOUNDATION
REV. MICHAEL J. GLASTETTER
BRAD VANDEVENTER

International Standard Book Number
0-9723933-8-2

TABLE OF CONTENTS

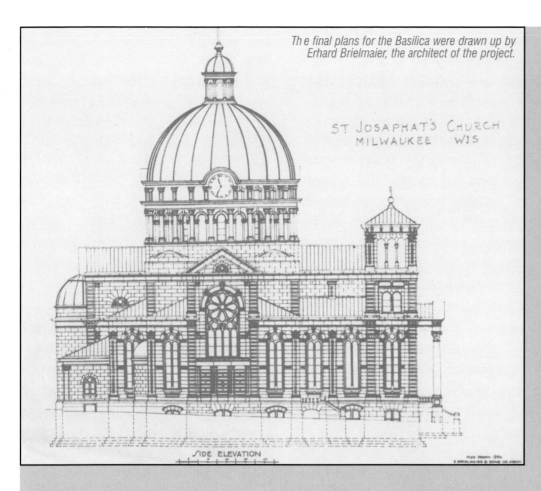

The final plans for the Basilica were drawn up by Erhard Brielmaier, the architect of the project.

The Beginnings

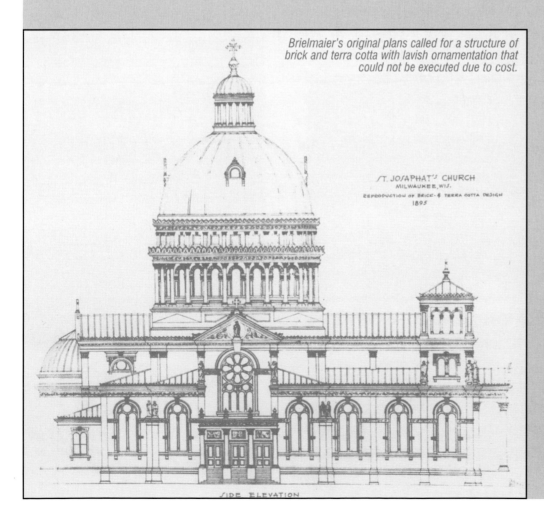

Brielmaier's original plans called for a structure of brick and terra cotta with lavish ornamentation that could not be executed due to cost.

There are many stories of how in moments of need, God provides. The history of the Basilica of St. Josaphat is one of those stories.

St. Josaphat Parish was founded in 1888 in a modest church on the southern border of the city of Milwaukee. Less than a year after it opened, a fire broke out in the church building and destroyed it. The parish quickly put up a new structure, a combination church and school, and the dedication took place on November 24, 1889 - but the excitement did not last long. The pastor, Rev. Wilhelm Grutza, soon realized the building was already too small for his growing parish.

In the late 1800s, Polish immigrants were pouring into the south side of Milwaukee. As the neighborhood swelled, St. Josaphat grew to become the largest parish in the city. Parishioners numbered more than 12,000 in 1896 when Archbishop Frederick Xavier Katzer directed the pastor to begin building another new church.

Father Grutza threw himself into the task. He dreamed of building a grand church, one the immigrant community would be proud of. So his first step was to contact Erhard Brielmaier, a prominent Milwaukee architect who specialized in ecclesiastical work. Brielmaier accepted the com-

History

The Post Office and Customs House as it appeared in Chicago (c. 1895). 200,000 tons of salvaged materials from this building were utilized in the construction of the Basilica.

Daring to Dream

mission and went to work.

The architect drew up plans for a classical-style building big enough to seat 2,300 people. The church would be made of brick, and the exterior would be graced with a terra cotta trim. On the inside, the design sought to minimize column obstruction and bring the congregation as close to the altar as possible. When the plans were made public, a journalist reported that the church "will not have its superior in the northwest, Chicago included." Whether the parish could come up with the money to build the church, however, was another question.

Providence Intervenes

The original estimate for the new church was $150,000 (roughly $3 million today). Father Grutza, undaunted, championed the project.

His determination paid off in 1895 when he found out that the Chicago Post Office and Customs House was slated for demolition. He got the tip from parishioner Samuel Reed, Sr., a stoneworker who had learned his trade on the Chicago building. The post office, which originally cost more than $4 million, was now being torn down because of severe structural flaws. Grutza made inquiries

and learned that the entire building - carved stone, granite pillars, wooden doors, ornamental bronze railings, light fixtures and more - could be purchased, packed up and shipped to Milwaukee for just $20,000. That was $30,000 *less* than the cost of new stone alone. Grutza consulted with Brielmaier, then quickly signed a deal.

New materials meant a new design, and this time Brielmaier faced an even bigger challenge. Essentially, he had to work backwards. Instead of drawing up plans and then ordering building materials to fulfill them, the architect now had to take existing materials and figure out what he could make with them. Like playing with blocks, but on a grand scale.

The Milwaukee contracting firm of Jesion & Dankert supervised the building demolition in Chicago and the transportation of the materials back home. During the spring of 1896, 200,000 tons of stone slabs, six granite pillars and other materials snaked their way north to Milwaukee. The complete shipment filled 500 railway flatcars. The materials were all unloaded by a spur track at the east end of the bridge where Lincoln Avenue crossed the Kinnickinnic River. From there, teams of draft horses pulled the materials to the building site. Each and every stone was then measured, catalogued and stored until needed.

An Immense Task

Work began in the summer of 1896. The first job was to remove the 30-foot hill that sat at one end of the building site. Father Grutza began the task by driving the first team and dumping the first load of earth. The men of the parish then joined in, digging with picks and shovels and hauling dirt away with horses and wooden wagons.

The next step was to lay the foundation. Because of the immense weight of the finished structure, Brielmaier wanted to make the foot-

Construction site facing south (c. 1898)

ings of the dome's eight piers as sturdy as possible. He imported Dyckerhoff Portland cement from Germany for the footings as well as the floor slabs and appointed one of his own sons to supervise the concrete mixing - ensuring the correct proportions of cement, sand and crushed stone was essential. (There were no large mixing machines. The parishioners at work on the project had to mix all the concrete by hand and transport it in wheelbarrows.) Brielmaier used steel rails to reinforce the footings and railway ties to strengthen the foundation.

In 1897, with the foundation and the basement complete, the parish needed a contractor to begin work on the building itself. As always, money was in short supply. To keep the work going and save money, Father Grutza decided to tackle the job himself. He became the mason contractor, supervising a crew of 30

workmen and saving the church over $30,000 (about $750,000 today).

As the building rose over the neighborhood, Brielmaier's second design began to take shape. The architect had envisioned a smaller version of St. Peter's Basilica in Rome. Above the cross-shaped floor, cranes spent months guiding the huge blocks of Ohio sandstone into place. Crews mortared the walls with domestic Portland cement. Paired bell towers went up above the facade and a skeleton of iron girders took shape above the walls to form the imposing dome. At 250 feet high and 80 feet in diameter, the new church's dome would be the fifth largest in the world. Only the domes of St. Peter's in Rome, the Duomo in Florence, the Capitol building in Washington and St. Paul's Cathedral in London were higher. Including columns, piers and footings, the dome of St. Josaphat Church

weighed almost four million pounds.

One of the laborers was injured in a fall from a scaffold, but he soon recovered. Another man was not so fortunate. Anton Kasprzyk, a Polish immigrant working on the church as a volunteer, was helping to unload a large stone from a freight car. The stone slipped and crushed him. He left behind a wife and seven children.

Triumph - and More Tribulations

In 1901, after five years of work, the building was finished, and on July 21 Archbishop Katzer celebrated a grand Pontifical High Mass to mark the dedication of the new St. Josaphat. More than 4,000 people attended the four-hour service, and a representative of Pope Leo XIII pronounced a papal blessing. St. Josaphat took its place as the largest and most magnificent of the Polish churches in the United States.

Grutza's vision had become a

DOME.
ST. JOSAPHAT CHURCH
MILWAUKEE WIS.

GNED BY
& SONS.
& SUPERINTENDENTS

CONSTRUCTED BY
THE J.G. WAGNER COMPANY
MILWAUKEE WIS.

Fr. Grutza, utilizing his skills as a blacksmith, saw to it that the dome of his church was constructed utilizing his skills with reinforced ironwork. It was the first of its kind in the United States.

Sacrifice and Success

reality - but at a high cost. Exhausted by the construction project and the responsibilities of his parish ministry, Father Grutza died a little more than a month after the dedication Mass. He was buried from the church and thousands attended his funeral. Their beloved pastor was gone, and the parishioners now had to face a new problem.

The original construction budget was $150,000. By the time the last doorknob was in place, the cost had grown to more than $400,000. Interest on loans and expenses was running double the parish income. In less than ten years, the debt grew to an overwhelming $750,000 - about $15 million in today's money. The immigrant parish was in danger of losing the beautiful church for which it had sacrificed so much. The debt went into receivership. Rumors flew

through the neighborhood. According to one, the church would become an opera house. Another said it would be turned into a theater.

The Franciscans Arrive

The Archdiocese had to do something about the staggering debt, so in 1908 Archbishop Sebastian Messmer began looking for a religious order to take over the parish. After several orders turned him down, he approached the Franciscan Fathers Minor Conventual. They agreed to accept responsibility for the parish, and in 1910 the first Franciscan pastor, Rev. Hyacinth Fudzinski, OFM Conv. arrived at the church.

During Father Fudzinski's four years of ministry, the parish cut its debt considerably, thanks in part to a $400,000 mortgage loan guaranteed by the Franciscans. Also, a number

of creditors agreed to accept payment of 25¢ on the dollar (those who waited, received their entire claim). The most heroic efforts of all, though, came from the parishioners themselves - many of them mortgaged their homes to help finance the debt.

In 1914 Rev. Felix Baran, OFM Conv. took over as pastor of St. Josaphat. He would remain at the parish for the next 28 years. With energy, capable administration and the help of determined parishioners, Father Baran attacked the debt problem anew.

One of those determined parish members was Valentine Jendrejczak, who led fundraising efforts. During one drive in the early 20s, Jendrejczak asked the people to donate one dollar for every year the Franciscans had been at the parish.

As the result of their generous response to this and other appeals, the massive debt was entirely eliminated by 1925. Freed at last from the burden of debt, Father Baran was ready to fulfill the final part of Father Grutza's vision - the decoration of the church's interior.

When the church was completed in 1901, the interior was painted alabaster white. In the years that followed, the parish added only a few decorative elements. Memorial stained glass windows arrived from Innsbruck, Austria, in 1901 and 1902. Professor J.S. Zukotynski of Chicago completed his grand mural of the martyrdom of St. Josaphat in 1904. When the time came for the complete interior decoration, Father Baran was determined that it be a work of great beauty.

In 1926 he commissioned Gonippo Raggi, a celebrated Italian artist, to create dozens of murals for the church. Baran also engaged the services of Conrad Schmitt Studios of Milwaukee to paint the ornamental plasterwork, finish the gold leaf frieze, and

Uncertainty and Hope

The interior of the church was originally painted alabaster white. Photographs of the dome (above) and north end of the nave (below) provide glimpses of this stark interior as it appeared in 1910.

paint faux marble on the columns. Thanks to Father Baran's careful management and more fundraising by Jendrejczak, no further debt was incurred during the decoration. The interior work was completed in 1928 - just in time for the great honor that lay ahead.

The Church Becomes a Basilica

On November 29, 1929, at a Pontifical Mass celebrated by Bishop Paul Rhode of Green Bay, St. Josaphat's was consecrated and elevated by Pope Pius XI to the dignity of a Minor Basilica. The ceremony of elevation took place on January 25, 1931, in the presence of His Eminence Samuel Cardinal Stritch,

the Cardinal Archbishop of Chicago and former Archbishop of Milwaukee. St. Josaphat was only the third church in the United States to be named a basilica.

The years that followed were exciting ones for the parish. In spite of the trials of the Depression years, the Basilica remained relatively debt-free and on a sound financial footing. In the late 1930s, Father Baran began planning for a new school - plans that were put on hold in 1940 when, on the day after Christmas, a fire broke out in the undercroft, or lower church. The blaze was sparked by defective electrical wiring, and it caused widespread

damage to the lower church and smoke damage to the paintings in the Basilica church. Father Baran recalled Raggi to supervise the restoration of the paintings.

When Father Baran died in 1942, the entire parish and many throughout the city mourned. His replacement was the Very Rev. Paul Czubaj, OFM Conv., who had served the Basilica for many years as assistant pastor. Father Czubaj's first task was to renovate and repair the undercroft. This included new fixtures, a new terrazzo floor, fresh paint and modification of the sanctuary and altar.

During a severe storm in the

After the razing of the school building on Seventh Street in 1977, the west side of the Basilica was fully visible from Lincoln Avenue for the first time. This photograph (c. 1988) shows the large patch on the north side of the dome needed to repair damage after a violent storm.

summer of 1947, lightning struck the dome, dislodged several large blocks of stone and hurtled them to the street below. Afterward, an inspection of the dome foundation and the church exterior showed that repairs were needed immediately. Father Czubaj began the project, only to hand it on in 1948 to his successor, the Very Rev. Bronislaus Swiszcz, OFM Conv. Illness forced Father Swiszcz to retire in 1951, and the new pastor and rector, the Very Rev. Gabriel Ignaszak, OFM Conv., completed the repairs that same year.

Father Czubaj returned as rector and pastor in 1957. He was succeeded in 1960 by the Very Rev. Bart Snella, OFM Conv., who died after barely one year in office. His successor was the Very Rev. Eugene Piasecki, OFM Conv.

Years of Change

These were years of growth and change in the Church at large and the Basilica. Under the leadership of the Very Rev. Constantine Zelinski, OFM Conv., who became pastor in 1963, the Basilica parish underwent

The interior of the Basilica as it appeared in the mid-1970s.

Coming of Age: Transitions

the liturgical changes of the Second Vatican Council. Father Zelinski, who espoused the minimalist theory of the period, called in Conrad Schmitt Studios to paint over the faux marble columns and much of the ornamental decoration. In the spirit of "less is more," the Basilica was redressed for the 60s. The parish also added a copper canopy to the Basilica from the sidewalk to the front door (it was removed in 1977).

More pastors came and went. The Very Rev. Ralph Vala, OFM Conv., replaced Father Zelinski as rector and pastor in 1970. The Very Rev. James Kowalski, OFM Conv., assumed leadership of the parish in 1972. He served until 1975, when the Very Rev. Anselm Romb, OFM Conv., came to the Basilica.

In 1976, a cleaning of the Basilica's exterior revealed the beautiful Ohio sandstone beneath a century of urban grit. The old school building was razed in 1977 and, for the first time, the western side of the church was fully visible from Lincoln Avenue. (Unfortunately, this was the side where Brielmaier had used all the ill-fitting and inferior stones, expecting them to be "hidden" by the three-story school.)

Father Romb's years at the Basilica ended in 1978, when he was elected minister provincial by the Province of St. Bonaventure. The Very Rev. Thaddeus Wiktorek, OFM Conv., took over as pastor.

Father Wiktorek was the first "native son" of the Basilica parish to assume the duties of rector and pastor. Like many of the pastors before him, he had his hands full with the building itself.

In 1986, a violent storm tore a piece of copper cladding off the dome. The dome was patched - about all the parish could afford was a "quick fix" - and Conrad Schmitt Studios came in to repaint the dome's interior. As Sacred Scripture points out, however, one should never sew a new patch onto an old garment lest it shrink and tear away. That is exactly what happened in 1989. The copper patch pulled away and the hole in the dome became worse - much worse.

Water began seeping into the ceiling plaster and started to cause serious damage. The Basilica's problems went beyond normal maintenance and upkeep. Without major repairs, much would be lost forever.

Interior restoration of the Basilica included the installation of solid oak and granite floors in 1997 (top and bottom).

Restoration

Restoring the Basilica

As in the past, the needs of the parish were much greater than the resources at hand. The first step was to commission a study of what needed to be done to save the Basilica. The Franciscans had to go begging even for the modest $20,000 to pay for this study.

The pastor at this time was the Very Rev. Michael Rozewicz, OFM Conv., who had succeeded Father Wiktorek in 1987. (Father Rozewicz was the second native son to become rector and pastor.) He asked the province for the money, but at the time the friars were experiencing a serious financial crunch of their own. They encouraged Father Rozewicz to appeal to the archbishop of Milwaukee for help. Since the Archdiocese of Milwaukee does not own the Basilica or its parish buildings, Archbishop Rembert Weakland, OSB was unable to provide direct financial assistance. He did, however, put Father Rozewicz in contact with several prominent Catholic businessmen of Polish ancestry. This group became the core of the St. Josaphat Basilica Foundation.

Established in 1991, the Foundation's first accomplishment was to hire Uihlein-Wilson Architects to develop a plan to save the Basilica. With Uihlein-Wilson, the Foundation determined that repairing the dome and doing other necessary upkeep would cost roughly $3 million.

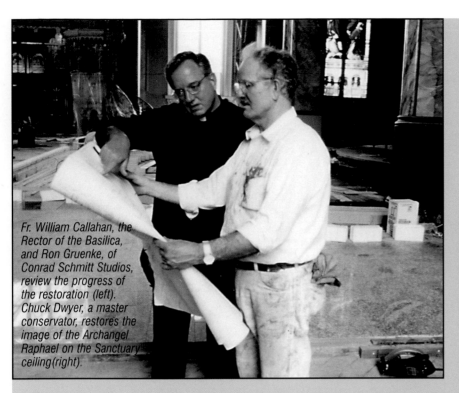

Fr. William Callahan, the Rector of the Basilica, and Ron Gruenke, of Conrad Schmitt Studios, review the progress of the restoration (left). Chuck Dwyer, a master conservator, restores the image of the Archangel Raphael on the Sanctuary ceiling(right).

Saving the Basilica

The project began in 1991. Hunzinger Construction Company did the exterior work with Christiansen Roofers working on the dome. Conrad Schmitt Studios replaced the old Plexiglas panels protecting the memorial windows with thermal pane shatter-proof glass. New boilers were also installed.

The work was finished in 1992 at a total cost of $1.5 million. Instead of the pale green cap that had become so familiar over the years, a gleaming brown copper dome now commanded the neighborhood. Structurally, the exterior was saved, but much work still remained inside the church.

With another province chapter coming up and the prospect of another change of administration on the horizon, momentum waned. In 1993, the Franciscans even considered leaving the Basilica altogether. Many in the order wanted to concentrate on other ministries. The Basilica

was big - with big problems - and few resources to draw from. Among those in favor of leaving was the Very Rev. William Patrick Callahan, OFM Conv. Another future, however, lay ahead for both the Basilica and Father Callahan.

Renewed Commitment

By a strange set of circumstances, God ignited once again in the Franciscan Province of St. Bonaventure the zeal for souls. The friars, with fewer numbers, decided to do the best they could in those ministries that were near and dear to their hearts. Since the Basilica parish was one of the oldest ministries in the province, the Franciscans reaffirmed it as one of their "core ministries." In other words, St. Josaphat would be one of the *last* ministries they would leave, even if their numbers were few.

The friar chosen to lead the Basilica parish at this important time was Father Callahan, and in 1994 Callahan - not a native son, not even

of Polish ancestry - returned as rector and pastor to the church where he had been ordained in 1977 and had spent the first year of his priesthood.

Thanks to the renewed commitment of the Franciscans, the Basilica Foundation found new energy. In 1995, with a $500,000 gift from Harry and Betty Quadracci, parishioners and friends of the Franciscans, the group began to work on a master plan for the church interior.

The Restoration

The Foundation's plan was simply to repair the interior. Father Callahan, on the other hand, envisioned a complete *restoration* of the Basilica's original 1926-1928 decorating scheme. He had long remembered a "tour" of the Basilica that Father Wiktorek had given him almost two decades earlier. As the two priests walked around the building, Wiktorek explained how the Basilica looked when he was a little

Ron Gruenke, of Conrad Schmitt Studios, guilds the orb and cross at the top of the dome with 23k gold in 1992.

boy. He was filled with love and tenderness as he talked about "his" Basilica. Father Callahan never forgot the mental images painted by Father Wiktorek. The inspiration of those images became the drive for the restoration.

The Foundation and the architects reasoned that limited funds demanded a much more modest project. Father Callahan argued for a full restoration. In the end, everyone agreed to see how the Basilica's columns would look with the original faux marble painting. Conrad Schmitt Studios was called in once more, this time to take up the same job the firm had done nearly 70 years before.

In June 1996, work began on Gonippo Raggi's murals. Thanks to the skills of Chuck Dwyer, a master conservator and artist, the beautiful paintings soon shown with new brilliance. The marbleization of the columns was eventually finished in December 1996. During the restoration project, the parish worshipped in the undercroft, but the removal of the sanctuary scaffolding in October

created enough room in the Basilica church for the October 26 wedding of Thomas Cullinan and Cynthia Moczynski. The reaction of everyone who attended was remarkable. It appeared that the restoration plan was a guaranteed success. As more was done, more of the original beauty of the church became evident, and enthusiasm for the project grew.

Attention turned to new light fixtures. As a newly ordained priest stationed at the Basilica in the late 70s, Father Callahan found one of the original Chicago Post Office light fixtures and hid it in the church attic. When discussion turned to new lighting, he knew exactly where to go for inspiration. Father Callahan climbed the attic stairs and retrieved the antique he had hidden almost 20 years earlier. At a planning meeting, he produced the treasure. By a remarkable coincidence, Steve Kaniewski of Milwaukee Brass Lighting Gallery also pulled out one of the originals. Even though the basic new electrical systems had been completed in 1992 during an earlier phase of the project, the good

work of Greg Rose from Roman Electric prevailed and new lighting was considered and funds became available. The Foundation approved the reproduction of the old fixtures.

Days of Glory

After nearly a year of work, the restored Basilica church opened in glorious splendor on March 30, 1997. The celebration was the Easter Vigil. As the lights gradually went up - starting with the Paschal Candle and building through a crescendo of full electric power - parishioners stood in awe as the very walls of their beloved church proclaimed New Life!

The Very Rev. Anthony Labedis, OFM Conv., Minister Provincial of the Province of St. Bonaventure, presided at a Mass rededicating the cornerstone of the Basilica on July 4, 1997. On July 16, the Feast of Our Lady of Mount Carmel, Archbishop Weakland offered a concelebrated Mass of Thanksgiving in the Basilica. The archbishop, a friend and supporter of the project, rejoiced with parishioners and the Franciscans in giving glory to God.

The Pope John Paul II Pavilion, the Basilica Visitors' Center, was dedicated in the Great Jubilee Year 2000. A statue of St. Joseph (left), patron of the restoration and renovation efforts, is located in the Donors' Chapel of the Pavilion.

Pope John Paul II Pavilion

New Growth

In the autumn of 1995, while discussing plans for the Basilica interior, Del Wilson, a partner of Uihlein-Wilson Architects, made a comment concerning the old boiler room. (The structure, a leftover piece of the original school building, was unused now that the heating system had been relocated inside the church itself.) Wilson offhandedly suggested to Father Callahan that some sort of structure be built to serve as a visitor entrance or visitor center. That idea took root in the mind of Father Callahan, and he never let it slip out of the plans for the Basilica. Michael Murry, the chairman of the Foundation board, rose to champion still another of Father Callahan's dreams. Eventually, the project evolved into plans for a completely new structure.

The original estimate for the new building was $800,000. As a proposed addition to a registered historic landmark, however, the plan had to be approved by Milwaukee's Historic Preservation Commission. The commission's requirements - cut exterior stone from the same Ohio quarry that supplied the old Chicago Post Office and install carved wood window frames and seamed copper roofs - added another $1.2 million to the cost. To help pay for the project, the Province of St. Bonaventure loaned the Foundation $1 million.

On September 13, 1999, in the presence of Archbishop Weakland, Milwaukee Mayor John Norquist and other dignitaries - as well as Ted Wieckowski and Julia Buczek, the two oldest living parishioners - the parish broke ground for the first new construction at the Basilica in nearly 100 years. As work progressed to completion, Father Callahan made a special trip to Rome to obtain permission to name the new building after the Holy Father.

Archbishop Weakland and Father Labedis dedicated the Pope John Paul II Pavilion on August 27 in the Great Jubilee Year 2000. The ceremony took place exactly one hundred years to the date after the funeral of the parish's founding pastor, Father Grutza. Through the rest of 2000 and 2001, the interior of the Pavilion was magnificently painted and decorated by classically trained master craftsman Andy DeWeerdt.

The Future of the Basilica

The Franciscans have ambitious plans for the years ahead. While the building renewal will continue with the renovation of the undercroft, the Basilica's "bricks and mortar" issues are for the most part taken care of. The Franciscans and the people of the Basilica parish now hope to devote more energy to their unique charisms - spirituality, community, optimism and hopefulness.

The friars hope to see the parish continue as a leaven of renewal within the surrounding neighborhood. Of course, as a vibrant parish church, it will continue as well in its mission to support people in their spiritual journey. As the friars remind parishioners from time to time, "The building isn't going to heaven - we are."

Very Rev. Felix Baran, OFM Conv., Second Franciscan Pastor and First Rector

Rev. Wilhelm Grutza, Founding Pastor

Wilhelm Grutza was born in Upper Silesia on January 8, 1856. A blacksmith by trade, Grutza was ordained a priest on June 24, 1887. He served as an assistant at Milwaukee's St. Stanislaus Church and was later chosen as the founding pastor of St. Josaphat Parish.

Fr. Grutza was a visionary, a man with big dreams and the will to make them a reality. He was also blessed with contagious enthusiasm, a quality that helped him convince the parishioners of St. Josaphat to embark on their grand building project. Grutza was praised as the "king of the bargain-makers" for the Chicago Post Office deal – a man who could "stretch a dollar until it did the work of five." He stretched himself as well, working tirelessly on the project and even supervising a work crew.

By the time the new St. Josaphat Church was complete, Fr. Grutza was exhausted by his labors – so much so that he was unable to take part in the great dedication ceremony on July 21, 1901. He watched from the side instead. After the ceremony, Grutza left Milwaukee for Denver in an effort to regain his health. He died August 20, 1901, at the age of 45. Fr. Grutza's body was returned to St. Josaphat Church, where thousands flocked to his funeral. He is buried at St. Adalbert Cemetery in Milwaukee.

Felix Baran came to America from Poland when he was a boy. In the United States, he entered the Conventual Franciscan Order and was ordained a priest in 1890. Before being named pastor of St. Josaphat Church in 1914, Fr. Baran served as pastor at churches in New York, New Jersey, Massachusetts and Connecticut.

Fr. Baran shepherded the parish through a time both difficult and exciting. When he took over as pastor, the parish was struggling under a huge debt. Thanks in large part to Baran's efforts, the debt was retired in just over 10 years. He also led the way on the decoration of the church's interior, bringing Italian artist Gonippo Raggi to Milwaukee to supervise the project. It was under Fr. Baran's leadership that St. Josaphat Church was named a basilica by the Holy See.

Fr. Baran was one of the best known and most loved priests in the Archdiocese of Milwaukee. He was called a "champion of the poor" because of his work with the St. Vincent de Paul society, and after his death in 1942, the Milwaukee Common Council praised him as an "outstanding churchman and humanitarian."

St. Josaphat, Patron of the Basilica

John Kuncevic was born in the early 1580s in a Lithuanian province of the Polish Kingdom. While still a child, he had a powerful mystical encounter with Christ – he felt a spark of fire leave Jesus' wounded side, enter his own heart and fill it with joy. In response to this experience, he began to memorize the psalms and ecclesiastical rituals and made plans to dedicate his life to the Church.

He entered the Basilian Monastery of the Holy Trinity in 1598 and took the name Josaphat. Ordained a priest in 1609, Josaphat immediately began serving the needy and homeless. He was also an excellent spiritual director, and under his influence over 60 men entered the Basilian order.

Josaphat was named the Archbishop of Plock (Plotsk) in 1617, a time of great conflict for the archdiocese. Originally the Ruthenians had been evangelized by the Byzantine Church from Constantinople. As the area came under the control of the Polish Kingdom (always Roman Catholic), the Ruthenians began to debate the idea of reuniting with Rome. In 1595 a Ruthenian Synod of Bishops voted to reunify with Rome under an agreement that allowed them to retain their Eastern rites. Josaphat worked tirelessly for the union's success.

Despite the agreement, major obstacles stood in the way of reunion – among them, Orthodox Bishop Meletius Smotrytsky and men sent to assist him from Constantinople. Slanders were spread about Josaphat and they tried to have him removed from Plock. In the face of persecution, Josaphat remained steadfast in his devotion to the Church and reunification.

His enemies, unable to remove him from office, turned to violence. While Josaphat was visiting the frontier town of Vitebsk, a mob attacked the mansion where he was staying and assaulted the inhabitants. Josaphat went out to meet them and said calmly, "Why are you attacking my servants? Take your anger out on me!" The mob attacked Josaphat viciously and threw his body into the river.

His death did not stop the Ruthenian reunification. Many miracles were attributed to him after his martyrdom. Perhaps the most amazing was the conversion of his attackers – Bishop Smotrytsky became a strong supporter of the Pope!

The Church canonized Josaphat on June 29, 1867. On the tercentenary of St. Josaphat's martyrdom, Pope Pius XI declared him the patron of reunion between Orthodox Christians and Catholics.

SW. JOZAFAT. B.M.

Erhard Brielmaier, Architect

Erhard Brielmaier was born in Wurtemberg, Germany, in 1841. His family immigrated to the United States when he was young and settled in Cincinnati. A builder's son and a self-taught architect, Brielmaier moved to Milwaukee in 1871 and established a practice that thrived for nearly 50 years.

The firm of Brielmaier and Sons designed and built many of the most beautiful religious structures in the city, including St. George Melkite Greek Catholic Church (1916), St. Benedict the Moor Catholic Church (1923), St. Mary's Convent and St. Joseph's Hospital (1929), and St. George Syrian Catholic Church. A gifted artisan in his own right, Brielmaier carved the beautiful wooden altars, pulpit and organ case at St. Anthony Church. The importance of Brielmaier's work was acknowledged in a 1986 exhibition at the University of Wisconsin - Milwaukee entitled "The Architecture of Yesteryear."

Biography

Self Portrait, by Gonippo Raggi

Gonippo Raggi, Artist

Gonippo Raggi was a native of Rome and a painter who specialized in the style of the Italian Renaissance. He came from a long line of artists, and as a boy learned much of his craft from his uncle, Alexander Raggi, then one of the most famous artists in Italy.

Gonippo was the outstanding student of the master of the Academy of Santa Lucia in Rome. In a design contest for the church of St. Cecilia Across the Tiber, Raggi's master beat 200 other artists to win the first prize of 10,000 lira. When the man died before completing the painting of the church, Raggi was chosen to finish the job. He became one of the most prominent artists in the country.

Raggi first came to the United States in 1907 to decorate the Basilica of the National Shrine of Our Lady of Victory at Lackawanna, New York (the second church to become a minor basilica in the U.S.). He also painted several churches in Boston, as well as part of the Vatican Palace after World War I.

While Raggi was working on St. Josaphat Church in Milwaukee, Pope Pius XI made him a commander of the Order of St. Gregory. After the fire of 1940, Raggi returned to the Basilica of St. Josaphat to supervise the restoration of the smoke-damaged paintings.

Coat of Arms of the Basilica of St. Josaphat

The shield is divided to signify the archbishop's pallium (stole). The shield has the following charges. The chief charge, required by Church law, is the papal insignia of the tiara and crossed keys of St. Peter, to signify the affiliation of our minor basilica to the major basilica of St. Peter in Rome. This is doubly fitting because St. Josaphat is buried there. The lower left is charged with the cornucopia (horn of plenty) from the coat of arms of the State of Wisconsin, to signify the prosperity of the New World, which the Polish immigrants hoped to find. The lower right is charged with the wounded heart of the young Josaphat, radiant with the sparks of divine love that he felt leap from the heart of the icon of the Crucified in his village church. The crest, required in a basilica coat of arms is the ombrellino (umbrella) of scarlet and gold, the original papal colors, which is carried in official processions. The supporters typically are a sign of membership in knighthood. Here the supporters derive from the coat of arms of the Order of St. Francis, the Order which serves the Basilica. The motto, "Ut omnes unum sint" ("That all might be one"), signifies Christ's high priestly prayer at the Last Supper in St. John's Gospel. As Christ prayed for the unity of His church, so St. Josaphat preached and died for that principle.

Coat of Arms of the Franciscan Order

The coat of arms has the crossed arms of Jesus Christ and St. Francis of Assisi with open palms bearing the stigmata or wounds. The Franciscan cord binds the arms together symbolizing the union of St. Francis with Christ through a life dedicated to the Holy Gospel and the vows of poverty, chastity, and obedience.

ART AND ARCHITECTURE
OF THE BASILICA the masterwork of many

The baldachino, an ornamental canopy supported by four columns, bears the Latin inscription *Ecce! Tabernaculum Dei cum hominibus!* (Behold! The dwelling place of God among men!). Its golden beauty reflects the precious mystery it contains. Beneath the baldachino is the High Altar in which the Real Presence of Christ in the Eucharist resides in the Tabernacle. Forming the base of the High Altar is a beautifully carved, high-relief marble representation of the Last Supper based on the famous painting by Leonardo da Vinci.

THE ALTAR OF SACRIFICE

Simple stone elements mark the historic and sentimental beauty and significance of the Altar of Sacrifice in the Basilica Church. The four onyx columns, originally part of the High Altar, were removed to reveal the carved masterpiece of Da Vinci's Last Supper. These columns, which match their counterparts on the Grand Pulpit, now support the *mensa* (table) of the altar erected during the renovations following Vatican II. The physical unity of the two altars, accomplished during the 1997 restoration, is meant to show the undivided strength of the Eucharist celebrated over the years in the Basilica Church.

The Eucharist is the heart of the Church and the focus for the Catholic community of believers. Christ has given the Eucharist—the Sacrament of His Body and Blood—to the Church for its sanctification until He comes again in His Glory. The Basilica Church is centered on this action of Christ. As we celebrate, so we live. As we live, so the Gospel is preached.

The insignia of the basilica includes a red and yellow striped *ombrellino*, or umbrella (top right) reminiscent of those carried over imperial and papal authorities and a *tintinnabulum*, or bell (top left) recalling those once used to signal the approach of a papal procession.

Stained glass window of the Holy Eucharist located in the west sacristy (bottom left) and an ornate gate of the communion rail (bottom right).

The Martyrdom of St. Josaphat (opposite, top), found directly behind and above the High Altar, was the first painting in the church. Painted by Professor J.S. Zukotynski of Chicago in 1904, the central figure of St. Josaphat is 13 feet tall.

In the central apse of the sanctuary is The Glorification of St. Josaphat (above), which was the first painting in the church by Professor Gonippo Raggi. Containing twenty-five figures, it depicts a glorious image of St. Josaphat entering heaven in the midst of angelic choirs and instrumentalists. Josaphat is greeted by the Lord Jesus on his right and the Blessed Virgin Mary on his left.

The four paintings on either side of the apse were painted by Raggi. On the east side (opposite, lower left) is St. Hedwig, Patroness of Poland, with selected Polish saints: St. Cunegunda, Bl. James of Strepar, St. Stanislaus, Bishop and Martyr, St. Hyacinth, and Bl. Bronislava. In the background is the city of Warsaw. The painting on the west side is The Miracle of the Vistula, commemorating the defeat of the Bolsheviks by the Poles on August 15, 1920 (lower right). The apostolic delegate to Poland, Cardinal Achille Rati (the future Pope Pius XI), prays to Our Lady of Czestochowa for victory. Cardinal Rati, upon his election to the papacy, was succeeded in Poland by Cardinal Lauri, a cousin of Professor Raggi. When Lauri returned to Rome from Poland in 1927, he prevailed upon his cousin to include The Miracle of the Vistula in the sanctuary.

Paintings immediately on either side of the Martyrdom were added in 1936. These depict St. Andrew Bobola, the Polish Jesuit killed by the Cossacks in 1657 (opposite, lower right) and St. Vincent de Paul, known for his works of charity among the poor in France (lower left).

the Lord as she learns that she is to conceive and bear a son. At the altar of the Annunciation, an image of Our Lady of Czestochowa is venerated. This image was painted by Ernest Galus, a parishioner who lived across the street from the Basilica most of his life. He died in 1987 at the age of 74.

THE SIDE ALTARS

There are four side altars in the Basilica. The two central side altars reflect a neo-classical Romanesque influence in keeping with the general style of the building. The altar of the Sacred Heart of Jesus (top right) depicts St. Margaret Mary Alacoque at Paray-le-Monial, France, where she was visited by Our Lord and asked to spread devotion to His Most Sacred Heart. The altar of the Annunciation (opposite, top left) shows Mary being visited by the Angel of

The two outer altars differ in style from the rest of the Basilica. More ornate and reflecting a Baroque influence, they are "survivors" of the original church, destroyed by fire in 1889. The altar dedicated to Our Lady of the Rosary (opposite, top left) is located on the east side

of the Basilica. The statue of Mary is flanked by statues of St. Apollonia, the patron saint of dentists, and St. Ignatius of Loyola, the founder of the Society of Jesus (i.e., the Jesuits). At this altar an image of Our Lady of Guadalupe is venerated. The altar on the far west side (top right) supports a statue of St. Joseph flanked by statues of St. Peter and St. Paul. This altar also features a sculptural representation of the Holy Family (bottom left) by Canadian artist Timothy Schmalz.

THE GRAND PULPIT

The commanding Grand Pulpit gives strong witness to the primacy of God's Word in the life of the Faithful. The pulpit is carved of white Italian marble. The cupola of the pulpit features the images of St. Florian (Patron of Firefighters), St. Hedwig (Patroness of Poland), St. Joseph (Patron of the Universal Church), and St. Anthony of Padua (Patron of Preachers).

Around the base, the image of Jesus the Good Shepherd is flanked by symbols of the four Evangelists: man (St. Matthew), lion (St. Mark), ox (St. Luke), and eagle (St. John). Most recently, images of St. Thérèse of Lisieux, Our Lady of Guadalupe, St. Jude, and St. Francis of Assisi have been added to replace original statues that were removed during the dressing-down of the Basilica in the 1960s.

I. Jesus Is Condemned to Death

II. Jesus Takes Up His Cross

III. Jesus Falls the First Time

IV. Jesus Meets His Mother

V. Simon of Cyrene Helps Jesus

VI. Veronica Wipes the Face of Jesus

VII. Jesus Falls the Second Time

VIII. Jesus Speaks to the Women of Jerusalem

IX. Jesus Falls the Third Time

X. Jesus Is Stripped of His Clothing

XI. Jesus Is Nailed to the Cross

XII. Jesus Dies on the Cross

XIII. Jesus Is Taken Down from the Cross

XIV. Jesus Is Placed in the Tomb

STATIONS OF THE CROSS

The fourteen marble carvings of the Stations of the Cross represent the route taken by Christ on the way to his crucifixion. Since 1342, when they took over custody of the Holy Places in Jerusalem, the Franciscans have been instrumental in the spread of this devotion. Because pilgrimage to the Holy Land was not possible for everyone, the Stations of the Cross were erected in churches throughout the world to enable the faithful to make a spiritual pilgrimage along the *Via Dolorosa* and meditate on the Lord's passion.

In the Basilica, the first seven stations are located in the east transept and the last seven are in the west transept.

STACYA X

Jezus z szat obnażony, octem, żółcią i mirą napojony.

STACYA XI

Jezusa do krzyża przybijają.

STACYA XII

Jezusa przybitego na krzyż podnoszą w górę.

STACYA XIII

Zdjąwszy Ciało Jezusowe składają na łonie Panny Maryi.

STACYA XIV

Jezusa do grobu składają.

East Windows

West Windows

Transept Windows (Above)
Gallery Windows (Right)

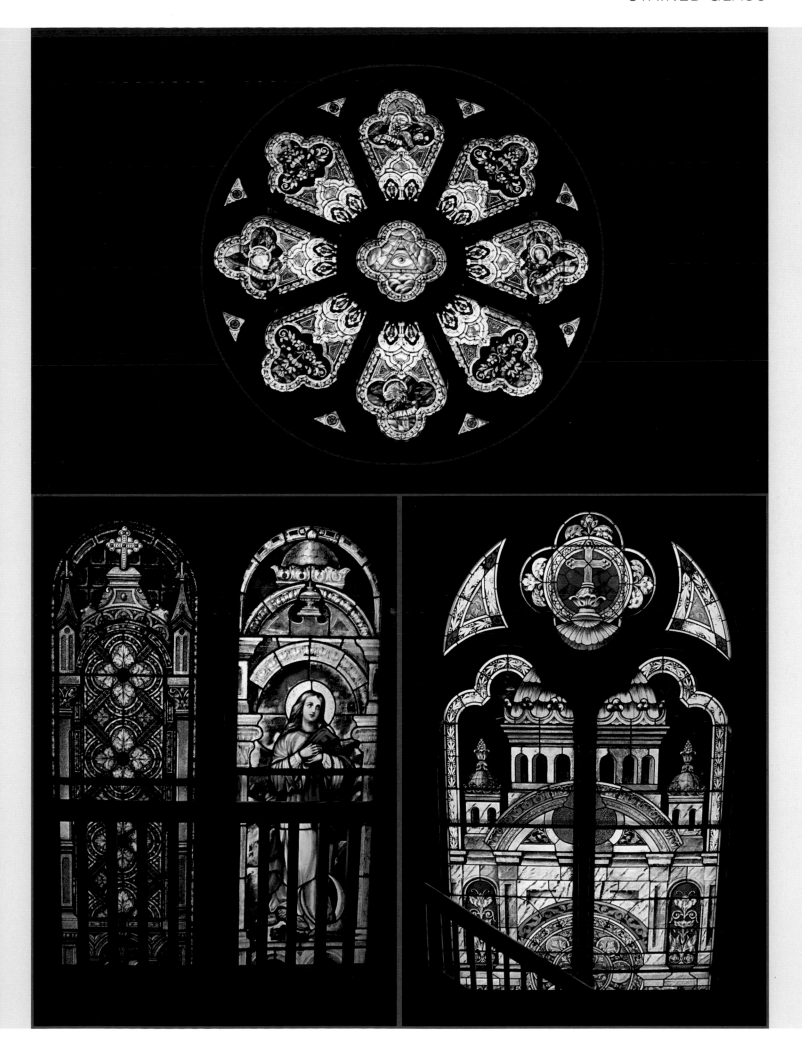

North Windows

Many of the stained glass windows were installed at the time of construction (1901-1902). The glass was imported from the Tyrolean Artists' Guild in Innsbruck, Austria.

East Side (p. 36)

Three windows of particular significance in Polish Catholic spirituality: St. Stanislaus, Bishop of Krakow, who in 1074 is reputed to have raised Piotrowin from the dead after he had appeared as a witness before Boleslaus II, King of Poland, over the rightful acquisition of ecclesiastical property (left); the apparition of the Blessed Mother with the Baby Jesus to St. Stanislaus Kostka (center); the death of St. Stanislaus, Bishop and Martyr, by the hand of Boleslaus II during Mass at the Church of St. Michael outside the gates of Krakow (right).

West Side (p. 37)

The appearance of the Sacred Heart of Jesus to St. Margaret Mary Alacoque (left); The Annunciation, the Archangel Gabriel tells Mary that she will bear a son by the power of the Holy Spirit (center); the

Agony in the Garden, the Archangel Chamael appears to Jesus (right). The stained glass fanlight above the door in the Basilica's west transept serves as the basis for the top and bottom borders of these pages.

Transepts (p. 38)

The large window in the

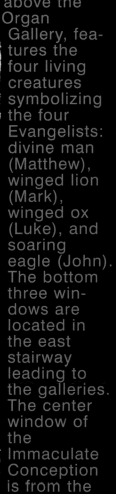

west transept (left) depicts the Nativity, the birth of Jesus. This image is flanked by images of St. Peter and St. Paul, the defenders of the Church. The rose window of this transept contains images symbolizing the four Evangelists surrounding a star. In the east transept, the large window (right) shows the Blessed Mother, with the Infant Jesus, presenting the rosary to St. Dominic while St. Catherine

of Siena looks on. This scene is flanked by St. Thomas Aquinas and St. Hyacinth. The rose window of this transept contains four images of six-winged Seraphim surrounding a crown.

Galleries (p. 39)

The large rose window (top), located above the Organ Gallery, features the four living creatures symbolizing the four Evangelists: divine man (Matthew), winged lion (Mark), winged ox (Luke), and soaring eagle (John). The bottom three windows are located in the east stairway leading to the galleries. The center window of the Immaculate Conception is from the original church destroyed by fire in 1889.

North Windows (p. 40)

Four windows depicting scenes from the New Testament: Jesus and the Children (top left), Woman Washing the Feet of Jesus (top right), The Resurrection (bottom left), The Descent of the Holy Spirit at Pentecost (bottom right).

The Franciscan Influence in the Mural Art

The great work of decorating the interior of the church was taken up during the term of Fr. Felix Baran, OFM Conv. (1914-1942). Fr. Baran, no doubt, understood the vision of Fr. Grutza, but with Franciscan devotion sought to enhance the interior's beauty with a glorious tribute to the life of St. Francis of Assisi.

The mural in the southeast quadrant **(1)** of the ceiling depicts the Saint and some of the early friars before Pope Honorius III. Francis presented his Rule for approval in 1223. The Rule and Life of the Friars Minor, essentially, is the Gospel of our Lord Jesus Christ.

The second stage of Franciscan life, depicted in the northeast quadrant lunette **(2)**, is a vision of St. Francis at the beginning of the Order as he was assured of its growth and intimate connection with the life of Christ. For St. Francis (and for Franciscans to this day), the Blessed Virgin Mary was Mother, Advocate, and Queen. St. Bonaventure notes in his biography of St. Francis that if the Church is to be restored, it must be conformed to Christ and to His Immaculate Mother.

The love of the Creator led Francis to a love and respect for all of creation. The next mural **(3)** reveals the image of St. Francis with a lamb that reminded him of the Lamb of God. Walking with one of the friars one day, St. Francis remarked about how Jesus, as humble as a little lamb, walked meekly and humbly among sinners.

To the northwest across the dome is the next image **(4)**. The evangelical or missionary aspect of the Order was paramount for St. Francis, so much so that he took up a mission himself to the Sultan of Babylon in a province of the Saracens. The event chronicled the bravery and courage of the Saint.

ST. FRANCIS

PAINTINGS

Next to this image is the mural that pays homage to the tradition that St. Francis and St. Dominic met each other on the way to Rome **(5)**. The pious legend centers itself upon the two Founders' extraordinary sense of love for the Church and their dedication to holy poverty. The legend holds that since neither had anything to offer the other, they exchanged belts. There is no evidence that the Founders actually met each other. Such legends, however, illustrate the gentleness of demeanor and love of God so dearly held in the lives of these two mendicants.

The next image introduces one of the most tender moments in the life of St. Francis **(6)**. It speaks of his great love for and awareness of the Incarnation. He receives the Child Jesus from the Blessed Mother. Francis is credited with the invention of the Christmas crèche in Greccio in the year 1223—the same year in which the Rule was approved.

In 1224, two years before his death, St. Francis ascended the heights of Mount La Verna and received the crowning glory of his life. The next mural **(7)** depicts Francis being marked with the sacred stigmata—the wounds of Christ in his own body. This event confirmed a life that was completely conformed to that of the Crucified.

The last mural **(8)** depicts the death of the Saint. As he was greeted by Sister Death, Francis blessed his beloved city and all of the friars, both present and absent. He was born to eternal life on the evening of October 3, 1226. The Feast of St. Francis of Assisi is celebrated October 4.

SIDE ALTAR LUNETTES

Gonippo Raggi painted four murals in the lunettes above the side altars.

(1) The beautiful painting of St. Thérèse of Lisieux entering heaven is above the Sacred Heart Altar.

(2) The mural of St. Dominic and St. Catherine with the Blessed Virgin is above the Annunciation Altar.

(3) The image of the Guardian Angel protecting a child is above the altar dedicated to Our Lady of the Rosary.

(4) The death of St. Joseph is depicted above the St. Joseph Altar.

Opposite:

An original oil painting of St. Francis of Assisi (1897) by Clotilda Brielmaier, daughter of the Basilica's architect, Erhard Brielmaier.

Before and After Restoration of 1996

The most characteristic feature of the Basilica of St. Josaphat is its magnificent dome. Representing the celestial heights, it immediately draws the eyes upward upon entering the church. The decoration of the dome is comparable to that of St. Peter's Basilica in Vatican City. The pro-portions of the eight sections are exactly the same, however those of St. Peter's are much larger. Wishing to use a similar color scheme, Raggi made much use of lapis lazuli and gold.

The very center of the dome is a window made of Eastern European crystal. The center of the window can be removed in warmer months to allow for air exchange through the windows at the base of the church.

The decoration of the dome represents Catholic faith in its magni-tude, starting from the beginning of time to the present. Surrounding the crystal center are

THE INNER DOME

representations of eight of the nine divisions of angels. Eight roundels depict Prophets from the Old Testament who predicted the coming of the Messiah. Eight lunettes containing paintings of Evangelists, Apostles, and Doctors of the Church complete the rotunda of the inner dome.

The drum of the dome features eight paintings depicting the seven Sacraments and the Adoration of the Magi. Separating these scenes are stained glass windows from Lucerne, Switzerland. These windows depict Mary, the Mother of Our Lord, and significant Polish and Eastern European shrines devoted to her.

The corona of the dome bears an inscription in Old Polish from 1 Kings 9:3 "I consecrate this house you have built, I place my name here forever; my eyes and my heart will be here for all times."

Top to bottom: Angel with Trumpet; Moses; St. Peter the Prince of the Apostles, Papal Coat of Arms, St. Paul the Apostle of the Gentiles; Adoration of the Magi

Angel with Violin; Prophet Elijah; St. Mark the Evangelist, symbol of the Winged Lion, St. Alphonsus Liguori; Sacrament of Matrimony depicted by the Marriage of Mary and Joseph

Angel with Pipe Organ; Prophet Isaiah; St. John the Evangelist, symbol of the Rising Eagle, St. Gregory the Great; Sacrament of Holy Orders

Angel with Scroll; Prophet Jonah; St. Bartholomew the Apostle, symbol of the Paschal Lamb, St. Jerome; Sacrament of Anointing of the Sick (Extreme Unction)

Angel with Trumpet; Prophet Amos; Apostle St. James the Younger, symbol of the Eucharist, St. Augustine; Sacrament of the Holy Eucharist depicted by the Last Supper

Angel with Violin; Prophet Daniel; Apostle St. James the Elder, symbol of the Monstrance, St. Thomas Aquinas; Sacrament of Reconciliation

Angel with Scroll; Prophet Jeremiah; Evangelist St. Luke, symbol of the Winged Ox, St. Ambrose; Sacrament of Confirmation

Angel with Tambourine; Prophet Joshua; Evangelist St. Matthew, symbol of the Divine Man, St. John Chrysostom; Sacrament of Baptism depicted by the Baptism of Jesus

The dome of the Basilica of St. Josaphat, the fifth largest in the world at the time of its construction, is larger than that of the celebrated Taj Mahal in India and Hagia Sophia in Istanbul. The cross on top of the Basilica's dome rises 250 feet above Lincoln Avenue (the height of a twenty-story building). Covered with copper and weighing over 1,500 tons, the Basilica's dome was the first structural steel dome in the United States. It is composed of an inner dome and an outer dome. The inner dome rises 204 feet above the floor of the Basilica and has a diameter of 80 feet.

IMIE MOJE BYŁO NA WIEKI, AŻEBY

BETWEEN THE DOMES

The dome is a double barrel vault construction with an inner shell separated from a higher outer shell. The space between the vaults varies from three to twenty feet and is crisscrossed by a skeleton of steel.

EAST BELL TOWER
LEVEL II

Originally rung by hand-pulled ropes, the Basilica's bells were mechanized in 1937 when motors connected to an electric timing device were installed. The remnants of that mechanism, shown here, give silent testimony to days gone by.

In September 1997, new swinging bell ringers were installed to swing the bells electrically. At that time, an electromagnetic striker system was also installed to toll the bells.

THE BELL TOWERS
LEVEL III

The bells of the Basilica, supported by steel and wood beams in the east tower, were purchased for the original parish church but never installed because they arrived after the devastating fire. The largest bell was consecrated "Sancta Maria," weighs 3,500 pounds and rings a 56D tone. "Sanctus Thomas Ap." is 1,800 pounds and rings 45F#, while "Sanctus Josaphat" weighs 900 pounds and produces a 34A. The three bells – Mary, Thomas, and Josaphat – have rung the time of day, tolled for funerals, and announced Masses for over 100 years.

Fr. Grutza, the blacksmith priest, saw to it that a bell was named after St. Thomas the Apostle. As the patron saint of builders, architects, stonemasons, and steelworkers, St. Thomas was seen as a special patron by the founding pastor.

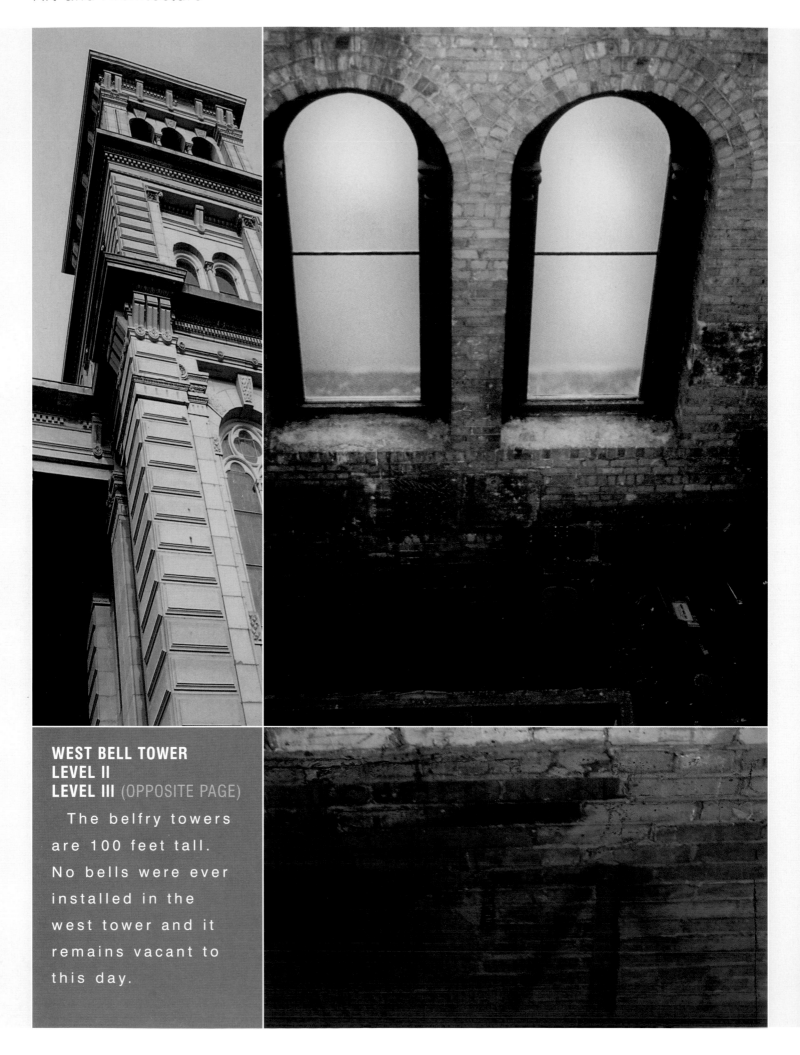

**WEST BELL TOWER
LEVEL II
LEVEL III** (OPPOSITE PAGE)

The belfry towers are 100 feet tall. No bells were ever installed in the west tower and it remains vacant to this day.

POPE JOHN PAUL II PAVILION

St. Francis of Assisi (opposite, top) an original bronze masterpiece designed by Bernard Gruenke, Sr. and produced in Rome by Domus Dei Sud Studios; original statues created in Rome of Sts. Peter and Paul (opposite, bottom left and right) commissioned for the Pavilion; crucifix in the Great Hall (opposite, bottom center) with 17th century corpus salvaged from the monastery of Monte Casino after World War II; statues of St. Anthony of Padua and St. Francis of Assisi (above, left and right); ceiling image of Archangel Raphael and portrait of Pope John Paul II (above, center) painted by Andy DeWeerdt in the Great Hall.

ORGAN GALLERY

EXTERIOR PHOTOS

The carved statue of St. Josaphat, Bishop and Martyr (opposite, top left) stands high above the main entrance to the Basilica. His watchful gaze shepherds the neighborhood below.

An ornamental doorknob from the original Chicago building bears the Great Seal of the United States Treasury Department (opposite, bottom right).

ST. JOSAPHAT BASILICA

This magnificent Temple of God is a monument of faith, erected by Polish immigrants at the close of the nineteenth century.
Raised to the dignity of a Minor Basilica in 1929 by Pope Pius XI, it was the third church to be so honored in the United States.
Its beauty reflects both the majesty of God and the devotion of its parishioners.

West Entrance, 2002,
Daniel Brielmaier

Postcards from 1915 (above) and 1909 (below)

St. Josaphat Basilica-
"The Church My Grandfather Built",
1976, Sr. Thomasita Fessler, OSF
-Courtesy of Haggerty Museum of Art